Keto

Chaffle Cookbook

for beginners

50 Quick, Easy and Delicious Chaffle
Recipes for Your Whole Family

Sophie Ross

TABLE OF CONTENTS

INTRODUCTION

Keto Diet is a high-fat, low-carb diet that is an increasingly popular way to lose weight. Keto is short for "ketosis", which occurs when the body has depleted its sugar stores so it burns stored fat instead of glucose in order to produce energy.

Losing weight on a keto diet sounds pretty easy; just eat a few bacon sandwiches and you'll be slimmer in no time. However, there are drawbacks to this diet, including very low levels of vegetables and fruit (so important for fiber and other nutrients) as well as constipation from lack of dietary fiber. Here are some tips:

- It's important to drink plenty of water, not only because you may be eating more sodium than you need, but because staying hydrated will help your body process proteins and fats more efficiently.

- For best results, stay away from most fruits and vegetables. Some berries are allowed; others aren't. Vegetables that are considered "low in carbs" or "leafy greens" are fine—but there is a difference between low-carb and high-fiber. As a rule of thumb, if it looks like it has the texture of tree bark or is covered with seeds or bulbs (e.g., artichokes), it probably has a lot of carbs and should be avoided.

- Be careful with spices, which tend to have a lot of sugar; salt is OK. It can be easy to go overboard on spices.
- Eat plenty of salmon, tuna and egg whites. Meat—including beef, chicken, pork and lamb—should comprise 20 to 25 percent of your total diet. (Be aware that "lean" meat is often not very lean. Be prepared to trim off most of that fat before cooking.) A little bacon or sausage is fine, too.
- Avoid condiments and sauces, including barbecue sauce and ketchup. These are full of sugar and other unhealthy ingredients.
- Drink mostly water (or unsweetened drinks such as tea or coffee). Try to avoid drinks with a lot of added sugar, like fruit juice or alcohol. If you choose to drink wine, go for the dry stuff—red wine is best.

Now, for Chaffles.

What is Chaffle?

Keto chaffle recipe is a versatile and easy-to-make low carb pancake that only requires 2 ingredients. It's a way to satisfy your sweet cravings while staying keto!

Chaffle is made from cheese and eggs. You will need grated cheddar cheese (use any kind of cheese you have on hand) and eggs, beaten together, then fried in a pan with butter or coconut oil.

Chaffles are perfect for a low carb breakfast, lunch or dinner and can be a treat right out of the pan, with butter!

Why Keto and Chaffle is a perfect combination?

Keto Chaffle is a great way to satisfy your sweet cravings while staying 100% in ketosis. It helps you feel fuller for longer but at the same time it's not a high carb treat.

Chaffle gives you a lot of energy and it's an easy way to prepare breakfast if you want it to be ready quickly when you get up or even if you're in a hurry so it can be prepared on the go without any issues.

Keto Chaffle tastes amazing plain, with butter or with any toppings you like and it can also be used as sandwich bread substitute.

Now, let us move to the recipe part.

BREAKFAST CHAFFLES

1. Creamy Cinnamon Chaffles

Preparation Time: 5 minutes

Cooking Time: 10 minutes

Servings: 2

Ingredients:

- Eggs: 2
- Shredded mozzarella: 1 cup
- Cream cheese: 2 tbsp.
- Cinnamon powder: 1 tbsp.
- Almond flour: 2 tbsp.
- Baking powder: ¾ tbsp.
- Water: 2 tbsp. (optional)

Directions:

1. Preheat your mini waffle iron if needed
2. Mix all the above-mentioned ingredients in a bowl
3. Grease your waffle iron lightly
4. Cooking your mixture in the mini waffle iron for at least 4 minutes or till the desired crisp is achieved and serve hot
5. Make as many chaffles as your mixture and waffle maker allow.

Nutrition: Calories: 582 kcal Protein: 33.93 g Fat: 44.06 g Carbohydrates: 12.09 g Sodium: 664 mg

2. Hot Ham Chaffles

Preparation Time: 5 minutes

Cooking Time: 10 minutes

Servings: 2

Ingredients:

- Eggs: 1
- Swiss cheese: 1 cup shredded
- Deli ham: ¼ cup chopped
- Mayonnaise: 1 tbsp.
- Dijon mustard: 2 tsp.
- Garlic salt: 1 tsp.

Directions:

1. Preheat your mini waffle iron if needed and grease it
2. Add egg, cheese, garlic salt, and ham a bowl and whisk
3. Cooking your mixture in the mini waffle iron for at least 4 minutes
4. Make as many chaffles as your mixture and waffle maker allow

5. Combine together Dijon mustard and mayonnaise and serve with the dip

Nutrition: Calories: 146 kcal Protein: 9.39 g Fat: 10.39 g Carbohydrates: 3.71 g Sodium: 2596 mg

3. Jalapeno Grilled Cheese Bacon Chaffle

Preparation Time: 15 minutes

Cooking Time: 20 minutes

Servings: 2

Ingredients:

- Egg: 2
- Mozzarella Cheese: 1 cup (shredded)
- Jalapenos: 2 sliced with seeds removed along with the skin
- Cream cheese: ½ cup
- Monterey jack: 2 slices
- Cheddar cheese: 2 slices
- Bacon: 4 slices cooking

Directions:

1. Add over two tablespoons of cream cheese to the half-cut jalapenos

2. Bake them for around 10 minutes and set aside
3. Preheat a mini waffle maker if needed and grease it
4. In a mixing bowl, beat eggs and add Mozzarella cheese to them and mix well
5. Pour the mixture to the lower plate of the waffle maker and spread it evenly to cover the plate properly
6. Cooking for at least 4 minutes to get the desired crunch
7. Remove the chaffle from the heat and keep aside for around one minute
8. Make as many chaffles as your mixture and waffle maker allow
9. Make a sandwich by placing a slice of Monterey Jack, a cheese slice, 2 bacon slices in between two chaffles and enjoy!

Nutrition: Calories: 295 kcal Protein: 11.23 g Fat: 24.4 g Carbohydrates: 10.68 g Sodium: 110 mg

4. Japanese Styled Breakfast Chaffle

Preparation Time: 5 minutes

Cooking Time: 10 minutes

Servings: 2

Ingredients:

- Egg: 1
- Mozzarella Cheese: 1/2 cup (shredded)
- Bacon: 1 slice
- Kewpie Mayo: 2 tbsp.
- Green onion: 1 stalk

Directions:

1. Preheat a mini waffle maker if needed and grease it
2. In a mixing bowl, beat an egg and put 1 tbsp. of Kewpie Mayo
3. Chop green onion and put half of it in the mixing bowl and half aside
4. Cut bacon into pieces of ¼ inches and add in the mixing bowl and mix well
5. Sprinkle around 1/8 cup of shredded Mozzarella cheese to the lower plate of the waffle maker and pour the mixture over it
6. Again sprinkle 1/8 cup of shredded Mozzarella cheese to the top of the mixture
7. Cooking for at least 4 minutes to get the desired crunch
8. Remove the chaffle from the heat and drizzle Kewpie mayo
9. Serve by sprinkling the remaining green onions

10. Make as many chaffles as your mixture and waffle maker allow

Nutrition: Calories: 277 kcal Protein: 16.17 g Fat: 22.82 g Carbohydrates: 3.32 g Sodium: 281 mg

5. Cinnamon Garlic Chaffles

Preparation Time: 5 minutes

Cooking Time: 10 minutes

Servings: 2

Ingredients:

- Egg: 1
- Mozzarella cheese: ½ cup (shredded)
- Garlic: ½ tbsp. ground
- Ground cinnamon: ½ tsp.
- Erythritol: 1 tsp. powdered
- Ground nutmeg: ¼ tsp.
- Almond flour: 2 tbsp.
- Baking powder: ½ tsp.

Directions:

1. Mix all the ingredients well together
2. Pour a layer on a preheated waffle iron
3. Cooking the chaffle for around 5 minutes
4. Make as many chaffles as your mixture and waffle maker allow
5. Serve with your favorite topping

Nutrition: Calories: 288; Total Fat: 24g; Carbs: 7g; Net Carbs: 4g; Fiber: 3g; Protein: 14g

6. Monte Cristo Chaffle

Preparation Time: 5 minutes
Cooking Time: 10 minutes
Servings: 2

Ingredient:

- For Chaffle:
- Egg: 2
- Cream cheese: 2 tbsp.
- Vanilla extract: 1 tbsp.
- Almond flour: 2 tbsp.
- Heavy cream: 1 tsp.
- Cinnamon powder: 1 tsp.
- Swerve sweetener: 1 tbsp.
- For Assembling:
- Cheese: 2 slices
- Ham: 2 slices
- Turkey: 2 slices

Directions:

1. Preheat a mini waffle maker if needed and grease it
2. In a mixing bowl, add all the chaffle ingredients and mix them well
3. Pour the mixture to the lower plate of the waffle maker and spread it evenly to cover the plate properly
4. Cooking for at least 4 minutes to get the desired crunch
5. Remove the chaffle from the heat and keep aside for around one minute
6. Make as many chaffles as your mixture and waffle maker allow

7. Serve with a cheese slice, a turkey, and a ham
8. You can also serve with any of your favorite low carb raspberry jam on top

Nutrition: Calories: 351; Total Fat: 36g; Carbs: 5g; Net Carbs: 4g; Fiber: 1g;

7. Zucchini Nut Bread Chaffle

Preparation Time: 5 minutes

Cooking Time: 10 minutes

Servings: 2

Ingredients:

For Chaffle:

- Egg: 1
- Zucchini: 1 cup (shredded)
- Cream Cheese: 2 tbsp. softened
- Cinnamon: 1/2 tsp.
- Erythritol blend: 1 tsp.
- Nutmeg: 1 tbsp. (grounded)
- Butter: 2 tsp.
- Baking powder: ½ tsp.
- Walnuts: 3 tbsp.
- Coconut flour: 2 tsp.

For Frosting:

- Cream cheese: 4 tbsp.
- Cinnamon: ¼ tsp.
- Butter: 2 tbsp.
- Caramel: 2 tbsp. (sugar-free)
- Walnuts: 1 tbsp. (chopped)

Direction:

1. Grate zucchini and leave it in a colander for 10 minutes
2. Squeeze with your hands as well to drain much water
3. Preheat a mini waffle maker if needed and grease it
4. In a mixing bowl, beat an egg, zucchini, and other chaffle ingredients

5. Pour the mixture to the lower plate of the waffle maker and spread it evenly to cover the plate properly and close the lid
6. Cooking for at least 4 minutes to get the desired crunch
7. Remove the chaffle from the heat
8. Make as many chaffles as your mixture and waffle maker allow
9. Whisk all the frosting ingredients together except for walnuts and give a uniform consistency
10. Serve the chaffles with frosting on top and chopped nuts.

Nutrition: Calories: 355; Total Fat: 25g; Carbs: 5g; Net Carbs: 4g; Fiber: 2g; Protein: 28g

8. Italian Bread Chaffle

Preparation Time: 15 minutes

Cooking Time: 20 minutes

Servings: 2

Ingredients:

For the Chaffle:

- Egg: 2
- Mozzarella cheese: 1 cup (shredded)
- Garlic powder: ½ tsp.
- Italian seasoning: 1 tsp.
- Cream cheese: 1 tsp.

For the Garlic Butter Topping:

- Garlic powder: ½ tsp.
- Italian seasoning: ½ tsp.
- Butter: 1 tbsp.
- For Cheesy Bread:
- Mozzarella cheese: 2 tbsp. (shredded)
- Parsley: 1 tbsp.

Directions:

1. Preheat a mini waffle maker if needed and grease it
2. In a mixing bowl, add all the ingredients of the chaffle and mix well
3. Pour the mixture to the lower plate of the waffle maker and spread it evenly to cover the plate properly and close the lid
4. Cooking for at least 4 minutes to get the desired crunch
5. In the meanwhile, melt butter and add the garlic butter ingredients

6. Remove the chaffle from the heat and apply the garlic butter immediately
7. Make as many chaffles as your mixture and waffle maker allow
8. Put the chaffles on the baking tray and sprinkle the Mozzarella cheese on the chaffles
9. Bake for 5 minutes in an oven at 350 degrees to melt the cheese
10. Serve hot and enjoy.

Nutrition: Calories: 181; Total Fat: 19g; Carbs: 4g; Net Carbs: 2g; Fiber: 2g; Protein: 1g

9. Peanut Butter & Jelly Sammich Chaffle

Preparation Time: 20 minutes

Cooking Time: 30 minutes

Servings: 2

Ingredients:

For Chaffle:

- Egg: 2
- Mozzarella: ¼ cup
- Vanilla extract: 1 tbsp.
- Coconut flour: 2 tbsp.
- Baking powder: ¼ tsp.
- Cinnamon powder: 1 tsp.
- Swerve sweetener: 1 tbsp.

For Blueberry Compote:

- Blueberries: 1 cup
- Lemon zest: ½ tsp.
- Lemon juice: 1 tsp.
- Xanthan gum: 1/8 tsp.
- Water: 2 tbsp.
- Swerve sweetener: 1 tbsp.

Directions:

1. For the blueberry compote, add all the ingredients except xanthan gum to a small pan
2. Mix them all and boil
3. Lower the heat and simmer for 8-10 minutes; the sauce will initiate to thicken
4. Add xanthan gum now and stir

5. Now remove the pan from the stove and allow the mixture to cool down
6. Put in refrigerator
7. Preheat a mini waffle maker if needed and grease it
8. In a mixing bowl, add all the chaffle ingredients and mix well
9. Pour the mixture to the lower plate of the waffle maker and spread it evenly to cover the plate properly
10. Close the lid
11. Cooking for at least 4 minutes to get the desired crunch
12. Remove the chaffle from the heat and keep aside
13. Make as many chaffles as your mixture and waffle maker allow
14. Serve with the blueberry and enjoy!

Nutrition: Calories: 175; Total Fat: 15g; Carbs: 8g; Net Carbs: 5g; Fiber: 3g; Protein: 6g

LUNCH CHAFFLES

10. <u>Pizza Flavored Chaffle</u>

Preparation time: 15 minutes
Cooking Time: 12 Minutes
Servings: 3

Ingredients:
- 1 egg, beaten
- ½ cup cheddar cheese, shredded
- 2 tablespoons pepperoni, chopped
- 1 tablespoon keto marinara sauce
- 4 tablespoons almond flour
- 1 teaspoon baking powder
- ½ teaspoon dried Italian seasoning
- Parmesan cheese, grated

Directions:
1. Preheat your waffle maker.
2. In a bowl, mix the egg, cheddar cheese, pepperoni, marinara sauce, almond flour, baking powder and Italian seasoning.
3. Add the mixture to the waffle maker.
4. Close the device and cooking for minutes.
5. Open it and transfer chaffle to a plate.
6. Let cool for 2 minutes.
7. Repeat the steps with the remaining batter.
8. Top with the grated Parmesan and serve.

Nutrition: Kcal 485, Fat 35g, Net Carbs 2g, Protein 26g

11. Maple Chaffle

Preparation time: 20 minutes

Cooking Time: 15 Minutes

Servings: 2

Ingredients:

- 1 egg, lightly beaten
- 2 egg whites
- 1/2 tsp. maple extract
- 2 tsp. Swerve
- 1/2 tsp. baking powder, gluten-free
- 2 tbsp. almond milk
- 2 tbsp. coconut flour

Directions:

1. Preheat your waffle maker.
2. In a bowl, whip egg whites until stiff peaks form.
3. Stir in maple extract, Swerve, baking powder, almond milk, coconut flour, and egg.
4. Spray waffle maker with cooking spray.
5. Pour half batter in the hot waffle maker and cooking for 3-minutes or until golden brown. Repeat with the remaining batter.
6. Serve and enjoy.

Nutrition: Kcal 390, Fat 27g, Net Carbs 3g, Protein 22g

12. Pumpkin Chaffles With Choco Chips

Preparation time: 15 minutes

Cooking Time: 12 Minutes

Servings: 3

Ingredients:

- 1 egg
- ½ cup shredded Mozzarella cheese
- 4 teaspoons pureed pumpkin
- ¼ teaspoon pumpkin pie spice
- 2 tablespoons sweetener
- 1 tablespoon almond flour
- 4 teaspoons chocolate chips (sugar-free)

Directions:

1. Turn your waffle maker on.
2. In a bowl, beat the egg and stir in the pureed pumpkin.
3. Mix well.
4. Add the rest of the ingredients one by one.
5. Pour 1/3 of the mixture to your waffle maker.
6. Cooking for 4 minutes.
7. Repeat the same steps with the remaining mixture.

Nutrition: Kcal 243, Fat 15g, Net Carbs 3.5g, Protein 22g

13. Walnuts Low Carb Chaffles

Preparation time: 10 minutes

Cooking Time:5 minutes

Servings: 2

Ingredients:

- 2 tbsps. cream cheese
- ½ tsp. almonds flour
- ¼ tsp. baking powder
- 1 large egg
- ¼ cup chopped walnuts
- Pinch of stevia extract powder

Directions:

1. Preheat your waffle maker.
2. Spray waffle maker with cooking spray.
3. In a bowl, add cream cheese, almond flour, baking powder, egg, walnuts, and stevia.
4. Mix all ingredients,
5. Spoon walnut batter in the waffle maker and cooking for about 2-3 minutes.
6. Let chaffles cool at room temperature before serving.

Nutrition: Kcal 492, Fat: 36g, Net Carbs: 3g, Protein: 35g

14. Holidays Chaffles

Preparation time: 10 minutes

Cooking Time: 5 minutes

Servings:4

Ingredients:

- 1 cup egg whites
- 2 tsps. coconut flour
- ½ tsp. Vanilla
- 1 tsp. baking powder
- 1 tsp. baking soda
- 1/8 tsp. cinnamon powder
- 1 cup Mozzarella cheese, grated

TOPPING

- Cranberries
- keto Chocolate sauce

Directions:

1. Make 4 minutes chaffles from the chaffle ingredients.
2. Top with chocolate sauce and cranberries
3. Serve hot and enjoy!

Nutrition: Kcal: 421, Fat: 21g, Net Carbs: 5.6g, Protein: 45g

15. Cherry Chocolate Chaffle

Preparation time: 15 minutes

Cooking Time: 10 Minutes

Servings: 1

Ingredients:

- 1 egg, lightly beaten
- 1 tbsp. unsweetened chocolate chips
- 2 tbsp. sugar-free cherry pie filling
- 2 tbsp. heavy whipping cream
- 1/2 cup Mozzarella cheese, shredded
- 1/2 tsp. baking powder, gluten-free
- 1 tbsp. Swerve
- 1 tbsp. unsweetened cocoa powder
- 1 tbsp. almond flour

Directions:

1. Preheat the waffle maker.
2. In a bowl, whisk together egg, cheese, baking powder, Swerve, cocoa powder, and almond flour.
3. Spray waffle maker with cooking spray.
4. Pour batter in the hot waffle maker and cooking until golden brown.
5. Top with cherry pie filling, heavy whipping cream, and chocolate chips and serve.

Nutrition: Kcal 468, Fat 39.5g, Net Carbs 2g, Protein 26g

16. Bacon, Egg & Avocado Chaffle Sandwich

Preparation time: 15 minutes

Cooking Time: 10 Minutes

Servings: 2

Ingredients:

- Cooking spray
- 4 slices bacon
- 2 eggs
- ½ avocado, mashed
- 4 basic chaffles
- 2 leaves lettuce

Directions:

1. Coat your skillet with cooking spray.
2. Cooking the bacon until golden and crisp.
3. Transfer into a paper towel lined plate.
4. Crack the eggs into the same pan and cooking until firm.
5. Flip and cooking until the yolk are set.
6. Spread the avocado on the chaffle.
7. Top with lettuce, egg and bacon.
8. Top with another chaffle.

Nutrition: Kcal 350, Fat 11g, Net Carbs 3.5g, Protein 34g

17. Sausage & Egg Chaffle Sandwich

Preparation time: 15 minutes

Cooking Time: 10 Minutes

Servings: 1

Ingredients:

- 2 basics cooked chaffles
- 1 tablespoon olive oil
- 1 sausage, sliced into rounds
- 1 egg

Directions:

1. Pour olive oil into your pan over medium heat.
2. Put it over medium heat.
3. Add the sausage and cooking until brown on both sides.
4. Put the sausage rounds on top of one chaffle.
5. Cooking the egg in the same pan without mixing.
6. Place on top of the sausage rounds.
7. Top with another chaffle.

Nutrition: Kcal 265, Fat 9g, Net Carbs 3g, Protein 26g

18. Choco Chip Chaffle

Preparation time: 20 minutes

Cooking Time: 15 Minutes

Servings: 2

Ingredients:

- 2 eggs, lightly beaten
- 1 tbsp. unsweetened chocolate chips
- 2 tsp. Swerve
- 1/2 tsp. vanilla
- 1/2 tsp. lemon extract
- 1/2 cup Mozzarella cheese, shredded
- 2 tsp. almond flour

Directions:

1. Preheat your waffle maker.
2. In a bowl, whisk eggs, Swerve, vanilla, lemon extract, cheese, and almond flour.
3. Add chocolate chips and stir well.
4. Spray waffle maker with cooking spray.
5. Pour 1/2 of the batter in the hot waffle maker and cooking for 4-minutes or until golden brown. Repeat with the remaining batter.
6. Serve and enjoy.

Nutrition: Kcal: 411, Fat: 15g, Net Carbs: 5.5g, Protein: 31g

19. Crunchy Coconut Chaffles Cake

Preparation time: 20 minutes

Cooking Time: 15 Minutes

Servings:4

Ingredients:

- 4 large eggs
- 1 cup shredded cheese
- 2 tbsps. coconut cream
- 2 tbsps. coconut flour.
- 1 tsp. stevia

TOPPING

- 1 cup heavy cream
- 8 oz. raspberries
- 4 oz. blueberries
- 2 oz. cherries

Directions:

1. Make 4 thin round chaffles with the chaffle ingredients. Once chaffles are cooked, set in layers on a plate.
2. Spread heavy cream in each layer.
3. Top with raspberries then blueberries and cherries.
4. Serve and enjoy!

Nutrition: Kcal 491, Fat: 36g, Net Carbs: 3.5g, Protein: 38g

20. <u>Coffee Flavored Chaffle</u>

Preparation time: 10 minutes
Cooking Time:7–9 Minutes
Servings:4
Ingredients:
Batter

- 4 eggs
- 4 ounces cream cheese
- ½ teaspoon vanilla extract
- 6 tablespoons strong boiled espresso
- ¼ cup stevia
- ½ cup almond flour
- 1 teaspoon baking powder
- Pinch of salt

Other

- 2 tablespoons butter to brush the waffle maker

Directions:

1. Preheat the waffle maker.
2. Add the eggs and cream cheese to a bowl and stir in the vanilla extract, espresso, stevia, almond flour, baking powder and a pinch of salt.
3. Stir just until everything is combined and fully incorporated.
4. Brush the heated waffle maker with butter and add a few tablespoons of the batter.
5. Close the lid and cooking for about 7–8 minutes depending on your waffle maker.
6. Serve and enjoy.

Nutrition: Kcal 571, Fat 45g, Net Carbs 8.2g, Protein 41g

DINNER CHAFFLES

21. Chicken Eggplant Chaffle

Preparation Time: 15 minutes

Cooking Time: 25 minutes

Servings: 2

Ingredients:

For Chaffles:

- Eggs: 2
- Cheddar cheese: ½ cup
- Parmesan cheese: 2 tbsp.
- Italian season: ¼ tsp.
- Chicken: 1 cup

For Eggplant:

- Eggplant: 1 big
- Salt: 1 pinch
- Black pepper: 1 pinch

Directions:

1. Boil the chicken in water for 15 minutes and strain
2. Shred the chicken into small pieces and set aside
3. Cut the eggplant in slices and boil in water and strain
4. Add a pinch of salt and pepper
5. Add all the chaffle ingredients in a bowl and mix well to make a mixture
6. Add the boiled chicken as well
7. Preheat a mini waffle maker if needed and grease it

8. Pour the mixture to the lower plate of the waffle maker and spread it evenly to cover the plate properly

9. Add the eggplant over two slices on the mixture and cover the lid

10. Cooking for at least 4 minutes to get the desired crunch

11. Remove the chaffle from the heat and keep aside for around one minute

12. Make as many chaffles as your mixture and waffle maker allow

13. Serve hot with your favorite sauce

Nutrition: Calories: 580 Fat: 50 g Net Carbohydrates: 2 g Protein: 30 g

22. Aromatic Chicken Chaffles

Preparation Time: 10 minutes

Cooking Time: 40 minutes

Servings: 4

Ingredients:

- Chicken: 2 leg pieces
- Dried bay leaves: 1
- Cardamom: 1
- Whole black pepper: 4
- Clove: 4
- Water: 2 cups
- Eggs: 2
- Salt: ¼ tsp.
- Shredded mozzarella: 1 cup
- Baking powder: ¾ tbsp.

Directions:

1. Take a large pan and boil water in it
2. Add in chicken, bay leaves, black pepper, cloves, and cardamom and cover and boil for 20 minutes at least
3. Remove the chicken and shred finely and discard the bones
4. Preheat your mini waffle iron if needed
5. Mix all the remaining above-mentioned ingredients in a bowl and add in chicken
6. Grease your waffle iron lightly
7. Cooking your mixture in the mini waffle iron for at least 4 minutes or till the desired crisp is achieved and serve hot

8. Make as many chaffles as your mixture and waffle maker allows.

Nutrition: Calories: 1396 kcal Protein: 114.74 g Fat: 99.7 g Carbohydrates: 4.23 g

23. Chicken Garlic Chaffle Roll

Preparation Time: 20 minutes

Cooking Time: 30 minutes

Servings: 2

Ingredients:

- Chicken mince: 1 cup
- Salt: ¼ tsp. or as per your taste
- Black pepper: ¼ tsp. or as per your taste
- Egg: 2
- Lemon juice: 1 tbsp.
- Mozzarella Cheese: 1 cup (shredded)
- Butter: 2 tbsp.
- Garlic powder: 1½ tsp.
- Bay seasoning: ½ tsp.
- Parsley: for garnishing

Directions:

1. In a frying pan, melt butter and add chicken mince
2. When done, add salt, pepper, 1 tbsp. garlic powder, and lemon juice and set aside
3. In a mixing bowl, beat eggs and add Mozzarella cheese to them with ½ garlic powder and bay seasoning
4. Mix them all well and pour to the greasy mini waffle maker
5. Cooking for at least 4 minutes to get the desired crunch
6. Remove the chaffle from the heat, add the chicken mixture in between and fold
7. Make as many chaffles as your mixture and waffle maker allow

8. Top with parsley
9. Serve hot and enjoy!

Nutrition: Calories: 926 kcal Protein: 72.1 g Fat: 58.74 g Carbohydrates: 33 g

24. **Pumpkin Chicken Chaffles**

Preparation Time: 10 minutes

Cooking Time: 20 minutes

Servings: 2

Ingredients:

- Boiled chicken: ½ cup
- Pumpkin puree: ½ cup
- Pepper: ¼ tsp.
- Egg: 1
- Mozzarella Cheese: ½ cup (shredded)
- Almond flour: 2 tbsp.
- Onion powder: a pinch
- Garlic powder: a pinch
- Salt: as per your taste

Directions:

1. Mix all the ingredients well together in a bowl
2. Pour a layer of the mixture on a preheated waffle iron
3. Close the lid and cooking for 5 minutes
4. Serve with your favorite sauce

Nutrition: Calories: 865 kcal Protein: 60.23 g Fat: 64.07 g Carbohydrates: 9.88 g

25. Garlicky Chicken Pepper Chaffles

Preparation Time: 5 minutes

Cooking Time: 10 minutes

Servings: 2

Ingredients:

- Egg: 1
- Mozzarella cheese: ½ cup (shredded)
- Garlic cloves: 2 chopped
- Pepper: ½ cup finely chopped
- Chicken: ½ cup boiled and shredded
- Onion powder: 1 tsp.
- Salt and pepper: as per your taste

Directions:

1. Mix all the ingredients well together
2. Pour a layer on a preheated waffle iron
3. Cooking the chaffle for around 5 minutes
4. Make as many chaffles as your mixture and waffle maker allow

Nutrition: Calories: 210 Fat: 9.3g Net Carbs: 1.3g Protein: 28.9g

26. <u>Sliced Chicken Chaffles</u>

Preparation Time: 15 minutes

Cooking Time: 25 minutes

Servings: 2

Ingredients:

- Egg: 2
- Mozzarella Cheese: 1½ cup (shredded)
- American cheese: 2 slices
- Chicken: 2 boneless slices
- Salt: ¼ tsp.
- Black pepper: ¼ tsp.
- Butter: 2 tbsp.

Directions:

1. Preheat a mini waffle maker if needed and grease it
2. In a mixing bowl, beat eggs and add shredded Mozzarella cheese and mix
3. Pour the mixture to the lower plate of the waffle maker and close the lid
4. Cooking for at least 4 minutes to get the desired crunch
5. Remove the chaffle from the heat
6. Add chicken, salt, and pepper together and mix
7. Fry the chicken in the butter from both sides till they turn golden
8. Place a cheese slice on the chicken immediately when removing from heat
9. Take two chaffles and put chicken and cheese in between

10. Make as many chaffles as your mixture and waffle maker allow

11. Serve hot and enjoy!

Nutrition: Calories: 268 Fat: 20g Net Carbs: 3.5g Protein: 13.8g

27. Ginger Chicken Cucumber Chaffle Roll

Preparation Time: 20 minutes

Cooking Time: 30 minutes

Servings: 2

Ingredients:

For Garlic Chicken:

- Chicken mince: 1 cup
- Salt: ¼ tsp. or as per your taste
- Black pepper: ¼ tsp. or as per your taste
- Lemon juice: 1 tbsp.
- Butter: 2 tbsp.
- Garlic juvenile: 2 tbsp.
- Garlic powder: 1 tsp.
- Soy sauce: 1 tbsp.

For Chaffle:

- Egg: 2
- Mozzarella cheese: 1 cup (shredded)
- Garlic powder: 1 tsp.

For Serving:

- Cucumber: ½ cup (diced)
- Parsley: 1 tbsp.

Directions:

1. In a frying pan, melt butter and add juvenile garlic and sauté for 1 minute
2. Now add chicken mince and cooking till it tenders
3. When done, add rest of the ingredients and set aside

4. In a mixing bowl, beat eggs and add Mozzarella cheese to them with garlic powder
5. Mix them all well and pour to the greasy mini waffle maker
6. Cooking for at least 4 minutes to get the desired crunch
7. Remove the chaffle from the heat, add the chicken mixture in between with cucumber and fold
8. Make as many chaffles as your mixture and waffle maker allow
9. Serve hot and top with parsley

Nutrition: Calories: 156 Fat: 6g Net Carbs: 5g Protein: 8g

28. <u>Spiced Chicken Chaffles with Special Sauce</u>

Preparation Time: 5 minutes

Cooking Time: 15 minutes

Servings: 2

Ingredients:

- Egg: 1
- Mozzarella cheese: ½ cup shredded
- Dried basil: ½ tsp.
- Smoked paprika: ½ tsp.
- Chicken: 1 cup boiled and shredded
- Garlic: 1 clove minced
- Salt: ½ tsp.

For the sauce:

- Mayonnaise: 1/4 cup
- Vinegar: 1 tsp.
- Sweet chili sauce: 3 tbsp.
- Hot sauce: 1 tbsp.

Directions:

1. Add egg, dried basil, smoke paprika, chicken, salt and cheese in a bowl and whisk
2. Preheat your mini waffle iron if needed and grease it
3. Cooking your mixture in the mini waffle iron for at least 4 minutes
4. Make as many chaffles as you can
5. Combine the sauce ingredient well together
6. Serve spicy chaffles with the sauce

Nutrition: Carbohydrates: 6 g Fats: 95 g Proteins: 47 g
Calories: 400

BASIC CHAFFLES

29. Fluffy Sandwich Breakfast Chaffle

Preparation Time: 5 min

Cooking Time: 3 min

Servings: 2

Ingredients:
- 1/2 tsp. Psyllium husk powder (optional)
- tbsp. almond flour
- 1/4 tsp. Baking powder (optional)
- 1 large Egg
- 1/2 cup Mozzarella cheese, shredded
- 1 tbsp. vanilla or
- Dash of cinnamon

Directions:
1. Switch on the waffle maker according to manufacturer's Directions
2. Crack egg and combine with cheddar cheese in a small bowl
3. Add remaining ingredients and combine thoroughly.
4. Place half batter on waffle maker and spread evenly.
5. Cooking for 4 minutes or until as desired
6. Gently remove from waffle maker and set aside for 2 minutes so it cools down and become crispy
7. Repeat for remaining batter
8. Serve with keto ice cream topping

Nutrition: Calories 188, Fat 9.8, Fiber 2.9, Carbs 5.7, Protein 25.1

30. <u>Keto Plain Chaffles</u>

Preparation Time: 3 min

Cooking Time: 6 min

Servings: 1

Ingredients

- small eggs
- 1/2 cup shredded cheddar cheese

Directions:

1. Preheat mini waffle maker until hot
2. Whisk egg in a bowl, add cheese, then mix well
3. Stir in the remaining ingredients (except toppings, if any).
4. Grease waffle maker and Scoop 1/2 of the batter onto the waffle maker, spread across evenly
5. Cooking until a bit browned and crispy, about 4 minutes.
6. Gently remove from waffle maker and let it cool
7. Repeat with remaining batter.
8. Store in the fridge for 3-5 days.

Nutrition: Calories 203, Fat 3, Fiber 3, Carbs 16, Protein 8

31. Vanilla Keto Chaffle

Preparation Time: 3 min

Cooking Time: 4 min

Servings: 1

Ingredients

- 1 egg
- 1/2 cup cheddar cheese, shredded
- 1/2 tsp. vanilla extract

Directions

1. Switch on the waffle maker according to manufacturer's Directions
2. Crack egg and combine with cheddar cheese in a small bowl
3. Add vanilla extract and combine thoroughly.
4. Place half batter on waffle maker and spread evenly.
5. Cooking for 4 minutes or until as desired
6. Gently remove from waffle maker and set aside for 2 minutes so it cools down and become crispy
7. Repeat for remaining batter

Nutrition: Calories 200, Fat 2, Fiber 1, Carbs 5, Protein 10

32. Crispy Sandwich Chaffle

Preparation Time: 3 min

Cooking Time: 4 min

Servings: 1

Ingredients

- 1 egg
- 1/2 cup cheddar cheese, shredded
- 1 tbsp. coconut flour

Directions:

1. Using a mini waffle maker, preheat according to maker's Directions.
2. Combine egg and cheddar cheese in a mixing bowl. Stir thoroughly
3. Add coconut flour for added texture if so desired
4. Place half batter on waffle maker and spread evenly.
5. Cooking for 4 minutes or until as desired
6. Gently remove from waffle maker and set aside for 2 minutes so it cools down and become crispy
7. Repeat for remaining batter
8. Stuff 2 chaffles with desired sandwich

Nutrition: Calories: 472 Carbohydrates: 1.2 Protein: 32.6 Fat: 42.4 Sugar: 0 Fiber: 0.4

33. Basic Keto Chaffle

Preparation Time: 3 min

Cooking Time: 4 min

Servings: 1

Ingredients

- 1 egg
- 1/2 cup cheddar cheese, shredded
- 1/2 tbsp. Psyllium husk powder
- 1/2 tbsp. chia seeds

Directions:

1. Switch on the waffle maker according to manufacturer's Directions
2. Crack egg and combine with cheddar cheese in a small bowl
3. Place half batter on waffle maker and spread evenly.
4. Sprinkle Chia on top, cover and cooking for 4 minutes or until as desired
5. Gently remove from waffle maker and set aside for 2 minutes so it cools down and become crispy
6. Repeat for remaining batter
7. Serve with desired toppings

Nutrition: Calories 189, Fat 3, Fiber 4, Carbs 14, Protein 7

34. Sandwich Waffle Chaffle

Preparation Time: 3 min

Cooking Time: 4 min

Servings: 1

Ingredients

- 1 egg
- 1/2 cup cheddar cheese, shredded
- 1 tbsp. almond flour (optional)

Directions:

1. Using a mini waffle maker, preheat according to maker's Directions.
2. Combine egg and cheddar cheese in a mixing bowl. Stir thoroughly
3. Add Almond flour for added texture if so desired; mix well
4. Place half batter on waffle maker and spread evenly.
5. Cooking for 4 minutes or until as desired
6. Gently remove from waffle maker and set aside for 2 minutes so it cools down and become crispy
7. Repeat for remaining batter
8. Stuff 2 chaffles with desired garnishing to make a sandwich

Nutrition: Calories 270, Fat 4, Fiber 10, Carbs 8, Protein 25

35. Flaky Delight Chaffle

Preparation Time: 3 min

Cooking Time: 4 min

Servings: 1

Ingredients

- 1 egg
- 1/2 cup cheddar cheese, shredded
- 1/2 cup coconut flakes

Directions:

1. Switch on the waffle maker according to manufacturer's Directions
2. Crack egg and combine with cheddar cheese in a small bowl
3. Place half batter on waffle maker and spread evenly.
4. Sprinkle coconut flakes and Cooking for 4 minutes or until as desired
5. Gently remove from waffle maker and set aside for 2 minutes so it cools down and become crispy
6. Repeat for remaining batter
7. Serve with desired toppings

Nutrition: Calories 83, Fat 1, Carbs 14, Protein 18

36. Keto Minty Base Chaffle

Preparation Time: 3 min

Cooking Time: 4 min

Servings: 1

Ingredients

- 1 egg
- 1/2 cup cheddar cheese, shredded
- 1 tbsp. mint extract (low carb)

Directions:

1. Using a mini waffle maker, preheat according to maker's Directions.
2. Combine egg and cheddar cheese in a mixing bowl. Stir thoroughly
3. Add mint extract and place half batter on waffle maker; spread evenly.
4. Cooking for 4 minutes or until as desired
5. Gently remove from waffle maker and set aside for 2 minutes so it cools down and become crispy
6. Repeat for remaining batter
7. Garnish with desired toppings

Nutrition: Calories 190, Fat 3, Carbs 18, Protein 11

37. Okonomiyaki Chaffle

Preparation time: 22 minutes

Cooking time: 11 minutes

Servings: 2

Ingredients:

- Mozzarella cheese: ½ cup
- Baking powder: ½ teaspoon
- Egg: 2
- Cabbage: ¼ cup (shredded)

Sauce

- Soy Sauce: 4 teaspoons
- Swerve/Monk fruit: 2 tablespoons
- Ketchup: 4 tablespoons (sugar-free)
- Worcestershire Sauce: 4 teaspoons

Toppings

- Kewpie Mayo: 2 tablespoons
- Beni Shoga: 2 tablespoons
- Green Onion: 1 stalk
- Bonito Flakes: 4 tablespoons
- Dried Seaweed Powder: 2 tablespoons

Directions:

1. Sauté a mix of chopped onions and finely cut cabbage and set aside.
2. Using a mixing bowl, another mix for the sauce containing all ingredients for the sauce and also set aside.
3. Quickly, preheat a mini-sized waffle and grease it.

4. In another mixing bowl, a mix of shredded Mozzarella cheese with cabbage, beaten eggs and baking powder.
5. Combine the mixture and pour into the lower side of the waffle maker.
6. With the lid closed, cooking for 5 minutes to a crunch.
7. Once timed out, take out waffles and serve in a plate.
8. Repeat process for the remaining waffle mixture.
9. Garnish the chaffles with beni shoga, bonito flakes, chopped onions and dried seaweed powder.
10. Pour the prepared sauce with Kewpie mayo. Serve and enjoy.

Nutrition: Calories 192, Fat 7, Carbs 13, Protein 11

38. Jalapeno Cheddar Chaffle

Preparation time: 12 minutes

Cooking Time: 5 minutes

Servings: 2

Ingredients:

- Egg: 2
- Deli Jalapeno: 16 slices
- Cheddar cheese: 1½ cup

Directions:

1. Preheat and grease a waffle maker. a mixture containing ½ half cheddar with beaten eggs, then mix evenly.
2. Sprinkle some shredded cheese at the base of the waffle maker, then pour the batter on the cheese and top again with more cheese with4 slices of Jalapeno.
3. With the lid closed, cooking for 5 minutes to a crunch.
4. Repeat the process for the remaining mixture.
5. Serve and enjoy.

Nutrition: Calories 262, Fat 4, Carbs 18, Protein 12

39. Basic Keto Chaffle Recipe

Preparation Time: 5 minutes

Cooking Time: 8 minutes

Servings: 1

Ingredients:

- 1 egg
- 1/2 cup cheddar cheese, shredded

Directions:

1. Turn waffle maker on or plug it in so that it heats and grease both sides.
2. In a small bowl, crack an egg, then add the 1/2 cup cheddar cheese and stir to combine.
3. Pour 1/2 of the batter in the waffle maker and close the top.
4. Cooking for 3-4 minutes or until it reaches desired doneness.
5. Carefully remove from waffle maker and set aside for 2-3 minutes to give it time to crisp.
6. Follow the Directions again to make the second chaffle.

Nutrition: Calories: 122, Fat:9g, Carbs: 5g, Protein: 10g.

40. Chocolate Chip Chaffle Keto Recipe

Preparation Time: 5 minutes

Cooking Time: 8 minutes

Serving: 1

Ingredients:

- 1 egg
- 1 tbsp. heavy whipping cream
- 1/2 tsp. coconut flour
- 1 3/4 tsp. Lakanto monk fruit golden can use more or less to adjust sweetness
- 1/4 tsp. baking powder
- pinch of salt
- 1 tbsp. Lily's Chocolate Chips

Directions:

1. Turn on the waffle maker so that it heats up.
2. In a small bowl, combine all ingredients except the chocolate chips and stir well until combined.
3. Grease waffle maker, then pour half of the batter onto the bottom plate of the waffle maker. Sprinkle a few chocolate chips on top and then close.

4. Cooking for 3-4 minutes or until the chocolate chip chaffle dessert is golden brown, then remove from waffle maker with a fork, being careful not to burn your fingers.
5. Repeat with the rest of the batter.
6. Let chaffle sit for a few minutes so that it begins to crisp. If desired, serve with sugar-free whipped topping.

Nutrition: Calories: 291, Fat: 25g, Carbs: 5g, Protein: 13g.

DESSERT CHAFFLES

41. Apple Pie Chayote Tacos Chaffle

Preparation Time: 15 minutes

Cooking Time: 50 minutes

Servings: 2

Ingredients:

For Chaffle:

- Egg: 2
- Cream cheese: ½ cup
- Baking powder: 1 tsp.
- Vanilla extract: ½ tsp.
- Powdered sweetener: 2 tbsp.

For Apple Pie Chayote Filling:

- Chayote squash: 1
- Butter: 1 tbsp.
- Swerve: ¼ cup
- Cinnamon powder: 2 tsp.
- Lemon: 2 tbsp.
- Cream of tartar: 1/8 tsp.
- Nutmeg: 1/8 tsp.
- Ginger powder: 1/8 tsp.

Directions:

1. For around 25 minutes, boil the whole chayote; when it cools, peel it and slice
2. Add all the remaining filling ingredients to it
3. Bake the chayote for 20 minutes covered with foil

4. Pour ¼ of the mixtures to the blender to make it a sauce
5. Add to chayote slices and mix
6. For the chaffles, preheat a mini waffle maker if needed and grease it
7. In a mixing bowl, add all the chaffle ingredients and mix well
8. Pour the mixture to the lower plate of the waffle maker and spread it evenly to cover the plate properly and close the lid
9. Cooking for at least 4 minutes to get the desired crunch
10. Make as many chaffles as your mixture and waffle maker allow
11. Fold the chaffles and serve with the chayote sauce in between

Nutrition: Calories: 77; Fat: 3g; Carbohydrates: 2g; Phosphorus: 67mg; Potassium: 194mg; Sodium: 229mg; Protein: 12g

42. Kiwi Almonds Chaffle

Preparation Time: 15 minutes

Cooking Time: 20 minutes

Servings: 4

Ingredients:

- Cheddar cheese: 1/3 cup
- Egg: 1
- Kiwi: ½ cup mashed
- Almond flour: 2 tbsp.
- Baking powder: 1/4 teaspoon
- Ground almonds: 2 tbsp.
- Mozzarella cheese: 1/3 cup

Directions:

1. Mix cheddar cheese, egg, lemon juice, almond flour, kiwi, almond ground, and baking powder together in a bowl
2. Preheat your waffle iron and grease it
3. In your mini waffle iron, shred half of the Mozzarella cheese
4. Add the mixture to your mini waffle iron
5. Again, shred the remaining Mozzarella cheese on the mixture
6. Cooking till the desired crisp is achieved
7. Make as many chaffles as your mixture and waffle maker allow

Nutrition: Calories: 221; Fat: 19g; Carbohydrates: 3g; Phosphorus: 119mg; Potassium: 140mg; Sodium: 193mg; Protein: 8

43. Rice Krispie Treat Copycat Chaffle

Preparation Time: 15 minutes

Cooking Time: 25 minutes

Servings: 2

Ingredients:

For Chaffle:

- Egg: 1
- Cream cheese: 4 tbsp.
- Baking powder: 1 tsp.
- Vanilla extract: ½ tsp.
- Powdered sweetener: 2 tbsp.
- Pork rinds: 4 tbsp. (crushed)

For Marshmallow Frosting:

- Heavy whipping cream: ¼ cup
- Xanthan gum: ½ tsp.
- Powdered sweetener: 1 tbsp.
- Vanilla extract: ¼ tsp.

Directions:

1. Preheat a mini waffle maker if needed and grease it
2. In a mixing bowl, add all the chaffle ingredients
3. Mix them all well
4. Pour the mixture to the lower plate of the waffle maker and spread it evenly to cover the plate properly and close the lid
5. Cooking for at least 4 minutes to get the desired crunch
6. Remove the chaffle from the heat and keep aside for around one minute

7. Make as many chaffles as your mixture and waffle maker allow

8. For the marshmallow frosting, add all the frosting ingredients except xanthan gum and whip to form a thick consistency

9. Add xanthan gum at the end and fold

10. Serve frosting with chaffles and enjoy!

Nutrition: Calories: 127; Fat: 7g; Carbohydrates: 10g; Phosphorus: 108mg; Potassium: 169mg; Sodium: 139mg; Protein: 7g

44. Coco-Kiwi Chaffles

Preparation Time: 5 minutes

Cooking Time: 20 minutes

Servings: 4

Ingredients:

- Cheddar cheese: 1/3 cup
- Egg: 1
- Kiwi: ½ cup finely grated
- Coconut flour: 2 tbsp.
- Baking powder: 1/4 teaspoon
- Coconut flakes: 2 tbsp.
- Mozzarella cheese: 1/3 cup

Directions:

1. Mix cheddar cheese, egg, coconut flour, coconut flakes, kiwi, and baking powder together in a bowl
2. Preheat your waffle iron and grease it
3. In your mini waffle iron, shred half of the Mozzarella cheese
4. Add the mixture to your mini waffle iron
5. Again, shred the remaining Mozzarella cheese on the mixture
6. Cooking till the desired crisp is achieved
7. Make as many chaffles as your mixture and waffle maker allow

Nutrition: Calories: 121 Fat: 8g Carbohydrates: 5g Protein: 4g

45. Rhubarb Almonds Chaffle

Preparation Time: 15 minutes

Cooking Time: 20 minutes

Servings: 4

Ingredients:

- Cheddar cheese: 1/3 cup
- Egg: 1
- Rhubarb puree: 1/4 cup
- Almond flour: 2 tbsp.
- Baking powder: 1/4 teaspoon
- Ground almonds: 2 tbsp.
- Mozzarella cheese: 1/3 cup

Directions:

1. Mix cheddar cheese, egg, rhubarb puree, almond flour, almond ground, and baking powder together in a bowl
2. Preheat your waffle iron and grease it
3. In your mini waffle iron, shred half of the Mozzarella cheese
4. Add the mixture to your mini waffle iron
5. Again, shred the remaining Mozzarella cheese on the mixture
6. Cooking till the desired crisp is achieved
7. Make as many chaffles as your mixture and waffle maker allow

Nutrition: Calories: 347 Fat: 16g Carbohydrates: 6g Protein: 45g

46. Strawberry Coconut Chaffles

Preparation Time: 5 minutes

Cooking Time: 20 minutes

Servings: 4

Ingredients:

- Cheddar cheese: 1/3 cup
- Egg: 1
- Strawberry: ½ cup finely chopped or mashed
- Coconut flour: 2 tbsp.
- Baking powder: 1/4 teaspoon
- Coconut flakes: 2 tbsp.
- Mozzarella cheese: 1/3 cup

Directions:

1. Mix cheddar cheese, egg, coconut flour, coconut flakes, strawberry, and baking powder together in a bowl
2. Preheat your waffle iron and grease it
3. In your mini waffle iron, shred half of the Mozzarella cheese
4. Add the mixture to your mini waffle iron
5. Again, shred the remaining Mozzarella cheese on the mixture
6. Cooking till the desired crisp is achieved
7. Make as many chaffles as your mixture and waffle maker allow

Nutrition Calories: 371 Fat: 36g Carbohydrates: 8g Protein: 4g

47. Almonds and Raspberries Chaffles

Preparation Time: 15 minutes

Cooking Time: 20 minutes

Servings: 4

Ingredients:

- Cheddar cheese: 1/3 cup
- Egg: 1
- Raspberries: ½ cup
- Almond flour: 2 tbsp.
- Baking powder: 1/4 teaspoon
- Ground almonds: 2 tbsp.
- Mozzarella cheese: 1/3 cup

Directions:

1. Mix cheddar cheese, egg, raspberries, almond flour, almond ground, and baking powder together in a bowl
2. Preheat your waffle iron and grease it
3. In your mini waffle iron, shred half of the Mozzarella cheese
4. Add the mixture to your mini waffle iron
5. Again, shred the remaining Mozzarella cheese on the mixture
6. Cooking till the desired crisp is achieved
7. Make as many chaffles as your mixture and waffle maker allow

Nutrition: Calories: 196 Fat: 108.g Carbohydrates: 13.4g Protein: 14.6g

48. Smores Keto Chaffle

Preparation Time: 15 minutes
Cooking Time: 25 minutes
Servings: 2
Ingredients:

- Egg: 1
- Mozzarella cheese: ½ cup (shredded)
- Baking powder: ¼ tsp.
- Vanilla extract: ½ tsp.
- Swerve: 2 tbsp.
- Pink salt: a pinch
- Psyllium husk powder: ½ tbsp.
- Dark chocolate bar: ¼
- Keto Marshmallow crème fluff: 2 tbsp.

Directions:

1. Create the keto marshmallow crème fluff
2. Beat the egg that much that it will become creamy and further add Swerve brown and vanilla to it and mix well
3. Now add cheese to the mixture with Psyllium husk powder, salt, and baking powder and leave chocolate and marshmallow
4. Mix them all well and allow the batter to set for 3-4 minutes
5. Preheat a mini waffle maker if needed and grease it
6. Pour the mixture to the lower plate of the waffle maker and spread it evenly to cover the plate properly
7. Close the lid

8. Cooking for at least 4 minutes to get the desired crunch
9. Remove the chaffle from the heat and keep aside for around one minute
10. Make as many chaffles as your mixture and waffle maker allow
11. Now serve the chaffle with 2 tbsp. marshmallow and chocolate bar

Nutrition Calories: 643 Fat: 51g Carbohydrates: 3g Protein: 41g

49. Rhubarb and Coconut Chaffles

Preparation Time: 5 minutes
Cooking Time: 20 minutes
Servings: 4
Ingredients:

- Cheddar cheese: 1/3 cup
- Egg: 1
- Rhubarb puree: ½ cup
- Coconut flour: 2 tbsp.
- Baking powder: 1/4 teaspoon
- Coconut flakes: 2 tbsp.
- Mozzarella cheese: 1/3 cup

Directions:

1. Mix cheddar cheese, egg, coconut flour, coconut flakes, rhubarb puree, and baking powder together in a bowl
2. Preheat your waffle iron and grease it
3. In your mini waffle iron, shred half of the Mozzarella cheese
4. Add the mixture to your mini waffle iron
5. Again, shred the remaining Mozzarella cheese on the mixture
6. Cooking till the desired crisp is achieved
7. Make as many chaffles as your mixture and waffle maker allow

Nutrition: Calories: 600 Fat: 10g Carbohydrates: 8g Protein: 30g

50. Strawberry Almonds Chaffle

Preparation Time: 15 minutes

Cooking Time: 20 minutes

Servings: 4

Ingredients:

- Cheddar cheese: 1/3 cup
- Egg: 1
- Strawberry: ½ cup mashed with fork
- Almond flour: 2 tbsp.
- Baking powder: 1/4 teaspoon
- Ground almonds: 2 tbsp.
- Mozzarella cheese: 1/3 cup

Directions:

1. Mix cheddar cheese, egg, strawberry, almond flour, almond ground, and baking powder together in a bowl
2. Preheat your waffle iron and grease it
3. In your mini waffle iron, shred half of the Mozzarella cheese
4. Add the mixture to your mini waffle iron
5. Again, shred the remaining Mozzarella cheese on the mixture
6. Cooking till the desired crisp is achieved
7. Make as many chaffles as your mixture and waffle maker allow

Nutrition Calories: 271 Fat: 19g Carbohydrates: 4g Protein: 27g

CONCLUSION

Ketogenic Diet is a pattern of the eating plan that is known to bring good results to many people. It does not use sugars or carbs and it consists of 70% fat, 25% protein, and 5% carbs. There are many foods which can be eaten on this diet plan.

It was developed as a treatment for neurological disorders and its benefits have been studied in treating epilepsy, autism, Alzheimer's disease (AD), mood disorders such as bipolar disorder (BD) and major depressive disorder (MDD), some forms of cancer including brain cancer, sleep disorders such as obstructive sleep apnea (OSA) and insomnia at different points in a person's life.

Ketogenic Diet was developed in the 1920s and is now gaining acceptance by medical community because of a growing body of evidence that correlates its use with improved management and treatment of cancer, epilepsy, Alzheimer's disease (AD), cardiovascular disorders, neurodegenerative disorders, mood disorders such as bipolar disorder (BD) and major depressive disorder (MDD) amongst others.

The diet has been used to treat children with epilepsy for a long time. It is useful in treating pediatric patients who have severe forms of epilepsy. Ketogenic diet is considered an effective alternative for children whose seizures cannot be controlled by medication or diet and are not responding to antiepileptic drugs.

Here are some more benefits of keto diet to inspire you more:

1. Ketogenic diet is a great diet for weight loss:

The Ketogenic Diet plays a major role in weight loss. It works by changing your body to fat-burning, so you lose lots of excess pounds while you are on the Ketogenic Diet. You will cut down on your sugar intake which can be one of the reasons for weight gain.

2. It helps to prevent cancer:

It has been reported that Ketogenic Diet can help prevent cancer from spreading in your body. It does this by reducing the growth of free radicals which are linked to cancer growth and tumor formation in body cells.

3. It helps to control seizures in epilepsy:

Ketogenic Diet is a great diet for people who suffer from seizures. It has been reported that the Ketogenic Diet can help reduce the number of and even eliminate seizures.

4. It keeps you satiated for a longer time and helps to treat obesity:

Ketogenic Diet puts your body in fat-burning mode so it keeps you satiated for a longer time, therefore helping you lose weight faster. This is especially helpful for people who have issues with cravings and binge eating.

4. It reduces inflammation in the body:

Studies have shown that Ketogenic Diet can help reduce inflammation in the body by eliminating excessive sugar from your diet. This is useful in preventing and treating a number of inflammatory diseases, including hypertension and diabetes.

5. **It helps with heart health:**

Heart disease is one of the leading killer diseases worldwide. If you are on a Ketogenic Diet, you will get high amounts of healthy fat which have been linked to heart health. Additionally, research has shown that Ketogenic Diet can help to lower your bad cholesterol levels, which can also be helpful for protecting against heart disease.

I hope with the help of these Keto Chaffle Recipes you will be able to start your Keto Diet in a healthy way. We all know that carbs can be fattening so these recipes will help you avoid that and lose some weight easily.

Thank you.